T0196058

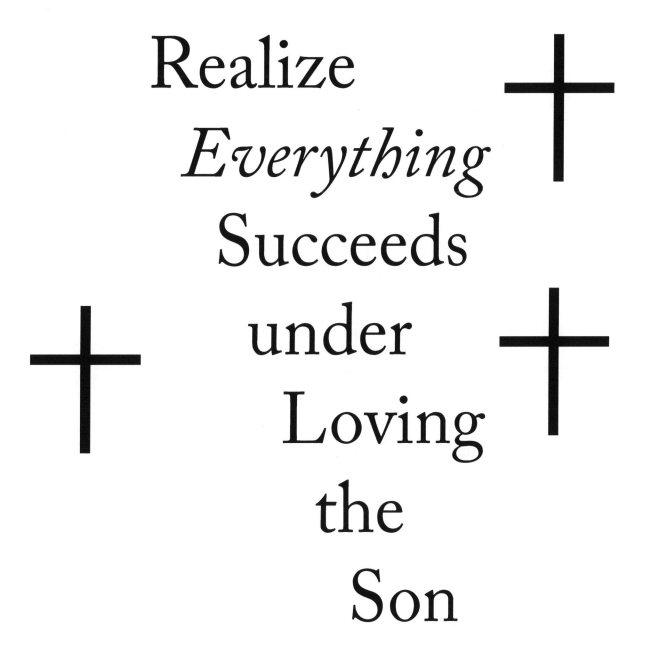

Realize *Everything* Succeeds under Loving the Son

Dr. Kenneth Harold McMillan

WESTBOW
PRESS®
A DIVISION OF THOMAS NELSON
& ZONDERVAN

WestBow Press books may be ordered through booksellers or by contacting:

WestBow Press
A Division of Thomas Nelson & Zondervan
1663 Liberty Drive
Bloomington, IN 47403
www.westbowpress.com
844-714-3454

Scripture taken from the King James Version of the Bible.

ISBN: 978-1-6642-0533-8 (sc)
ISBN: 978-1-6642-0532-1 (e)

Library of Congress Control Number: 2020917599

Print information available on the last page.

WestBow Press rev. date: 10/02/2020

Contents

Author's Note

T HE FRONT COVER represents decisions that everybody must make. The center cross represents the lovingkindness of our Lord and Savior, Jesus Christ, who died for our sins—the greatest miracle and gift the world has ever received.

Have you noticed the other two crosses to the left and right of the center? One represents mankind's decision to accept responsibility for erroneous actions and sins. Mankind accepted Jesus Christ as Lord and Savior at that time and place. The other cross represents mankind's indecision to not accept responsibility for erroneous actions and to not accept God's gift of salvation. We must pity the souls of those who chose this path. So many people have the opportunity, but they never accept Jesus.

Preface

Is there a goal or mission in life that you feel compelled to achieve? Has the Lord placed an objective in your heart? When I asked myself those very poignant questions, I had very few responses. I believe with every fiber of my being that we all have a purpose, a mission, and a calling to do something for the Lord. When we understand that God is really calling all believers to enhance His kingdom, do we ever ask Him: What is my personal role in all of this?

I have been a pastor for more than sixteen years and preach and teach in a Bible-believing, Jesus Christ-loving evangelistic church. We believe the Holy scriptures are the inherent, infallible, undeniable, life-giving, heart-changing Word of God.

The personal mantra by which I live is: I do not do anything Half-heartedly, make Excuses, have a Lying tongue, or bask in Laziness (HELL). The Lord created the Link Baptist Church to be a church that would connect and lead this generation back to God. We are an evangelistic, discipleship church because we have a strong desire to see souls saved and believe God has given us a mission, vision, and purpose in achieving *results*. We believe in the whole counsel of God and desire to be living epistles that the Lord Jesus is sending out to the world as proclaimers of His Good News.

After a good season of a few years of learning and teaching, we desire to see God's will in our lives and in the lives of others. We hold ourselves accountable—the reason for the birth of this book: *results*. We pray that this book will be beneficial to you as you advance in Christian discipleship and in your Christian walk. We also pray that the book will aid you in attaining desired *results* in your Christian walk. We know that to obtain His *results*, we must *trust God* and *follow Jesus.*

The Lazy Church

THE CHARACTERISTICS OF a lazy church are many. The lazy church is inactive, underactive, sluggish, and slow to act. Doing things well is not a part of its agenda. Little to no accountability is required. Excuses are prevalent. Laziness hurts the witness for Jesus. It damages relationships with other believers and wastes time and God-given gifts.

People deem the lazy church as unreliable or untrustworthy. Procrastination is a characteristic that is an enemy to reliability and trustworthiness. Delaying the initiation of a promised project or action without communicating a valid reason yields untrustworthiness. Another aspect of the lazy church is starting projects and noting reasons not to finish. We should never be haphazard and incomplete about God's assignments because exhibiting careless, irresponsible, and neglectful behavior is not Christlike and does not yield desired results.

After Paul's conversion, he dedicated the rest of his life training church leaders. He was adamant about the work *of* the church and the work *in* the church. He was results-oriented, and we must be likewise.

Food for Thought

Laziness has no place in the church.

Life Application

How would you classify the church where you hold membership? Lazy? Not lazy? Vibrant? Not vibrant? Other? Explain. _____

_____

_____

Salvation, Justification, Sanctification, and Glorification

These four terms are interconnected. Salvation is directly tied to justification. Salvation is when Jesus, Lord and Savior, saves our souls eternally from the devil's hell. Salvation, therefore, is directly tied to justification. Justification is when God declares us righteous. We are justified because we believe in God and accept the shed blood of the Lord Jesus. Salvation and justification lead to sanctification. Sanctification comes after one has been saved. Sanctification occurs when God sets us apart for His service. Thus, salvation, justification, and sanctification are interconnected and will eventually lead to glorification. When we achieve glorification, we acquire a glorified body, a body that cannot become sick or die. So glorification and sanctification are directly connected. All are pathways on the spiritual pilgrimage.

Read the following scriptures.

- Romans 3:10
- Romans 5:12
- Romans 6:23
- Romans 5:8
- Ephesians 2:8–9

Salvation is freedom from the penalty of sin. It is acquired through faith. Thus it is not about how good one is because no one is righteous; everyone has done or said something wrong. God intended for humankind to live forever, but because Adam, the first man created by God, sinned, death came on the scene.

Even though we die naturally, the good news is that Jesus Christ, the Son of God, made it possible for us to live forever in the spiritual realm. God loves us so much that He sacrificed His only Son, Jesus Christ, on the cross for all our sins and made it possible for us to live forever in the spiritual realm. This was a demonstration of agape love, the highest form of love. Eternal life is God's gift to us. He did not have to do it, but He did! He made a way for us; He gave us a way out! As aforementioned, salvation is acquired through faith, but grace makes it possible. Biblical faith and biblical works make God's grace more visible in our lives and enable us to be points of light in the world for Jesus.

Specifically, salvation is acquired by having faith in the finished work of Jesus Christ and through the confession of our sins. The finished work of Jesus Christ was established at the cross on Calvary when Jesus died for the sins of humankind. This is where Jesus paid our sin debt forever in full. However, we must repent for our personal sins. We must pray for forgiveness for things that we have done but should not have and for things we should have done but did not. Repentance is the personal, absolute, ultimate, and unconditional surrender to God's holy sovereignty.

When repenting, we confess our sins. We turn away from our old ways and turn toward Jesus and His ways. It is a complete change in direction in life and in decision making. Unfortunately, people often confess and repent for an offense because of a perceived outcome and do not make a lifestyle change. For instance, you know you are wrong, and you say you are sorry only to avoid the consequences of your actions. However, you continue to live in sin.

Food for Thought

All phases of the Christian journey are needed to reach the desired results.

Life Application

Reflect on your salvation experience. _____
_____
_____

How would you lead someone in a prayer of repentance? _____
_____
_____

Read the following scriptures.

- 1 Peter 1:15–16
- Acts 26:16–18
- Romans 8:30

God requires sanctification, the process of being set apart for service to God alone. God's directive is that His followers live holy lives. Saul, the chief persecutor of Christians, received a name change when He was called by God. He was converted to Christianity and set apart for service to God for the purpose of ministering, witnessing, teaching, and leading people to Christ.

God is omnipotent; He is all powerful. He can do whatever He wants at any given time; God never has to ask our permission. Remember that God is sovereign and holy. He calls, and we follow. Trust God and follow Jesus. As believers, we are duty bound in this faith walk, following our Lord and Savior, Jesus Christ. Thus God calls and justifies whomever He chooses, just as He called and justified Saul in these scriptures. In doing so, He validated that Saul, the sinner, was in right standing with Him.

Life Application

Respond to the questions below.

Is God calling me? _____
_____

Am I listening? _____

Do I hear God? _____

If God is calling and I am listening, what is He saying? _____
_____
_____

Read the following scriptures.

- Titus 3:7
- Romans 5:1
- Galatians 2:16
- 1 Thessalonians 4:5
- 1 Corinthians 6:9–11
- 1 Thessalonians 5:23
- 1 Thessalonians 4:16–17

Christians such as Paul received justification through grace. We are also justified by faith. We cannot work our way into justification. After his conversion, Paul became a highly devout teacher of Christianity, emphasizing sanctification as he knew it was important to God. Thus he incorporated sanctification in his curriculum and taught it everywhere he went. Being a great role model, he applied his teachings to his life and referred to his walk on many occasions. He also reminded those under his tutelage of his former teachings. To the people of Thessalonica, he stated,

Paul knew human behavior and what was unacceptable to God. His teachings were more about living a disciplined life after conversion. He stressed the importance of sanctification to the Corinthians (1 Corinthians 1:14–18). Paul knew it was easy to fall back into the old ways of life, so he reminded the Corinthians that they had been called to walk uprightly in their new life in Christ Jesus. His teachings addressed the whole person—spirit, soul, and body. In concluding a message to the Thessalonians, he prayed for peace and sanctification.

Sanctification is a process. Throughout our lives, we, as Christians, should be continuously refining our walk with Christ in order to be more like Him. Christlikeness should be the goal of every Christian. When we look in the mirror, we should desire to see more of Him. When we see more of Him, we see results.

When Saul was converted, the Lord used him in his new personhood—Paul—to establish several churches and lead people to Christ. Paul shared names of individuals he led to Christ. Paul indicated that his focus was not on whom he baptized but on his purpose, to preach the good news of Jesus Christ.

It is evident that Paul had a personal relationship with Christ, and he fulfilled his purpose and achieved results. Thus, if we want to fulfill our purpose in life and achieve results, we also must have personal relationships with Christ. Paul, with the help of God, accomplished much. Besides establishing the church, he authored several books of the New Testament.

Life Application

Reflect on your sanctification process. _____
_____
_____
_____

Do you know your purpose? Explain. _____
_____
_____
_____

What results have you obtained in your Christian walk? _____
_____
_____
_____

Read the following scriptures.

- Psalm 49:15
- 1 Thessalonians 4:16–17
- 1 John 3:2
- Revelation 21:4
- Revelation 22:1–5
- Romans 8:18
- 1 Peter 5:4

The day will come when we will be called from labor to reward and into rest until the first trumpet sounds, unless we are still alive when Jesus comes back for His church. If we are in the grave at the time of the first trumpet, it will be no problem for God because He will call us from the grave. According to the Bible, the scene will be awesome. Glorification is the end of the spiritual pilgrimage. It is a process of replacing mortality with immortality. Everything will be lovely and peaceful. The cares of this world will be no more. Glorification is the phase of the Christian journey when there are no worries or concerns. Everything imaginable and unimaginable will be available. This life is no comparison to the life we will have with Christ for eternity. What a day of rejoicing it will be!

Self

SELF-PRESERVATION INVOLVES BEING in total control in terms of protecting oneself. From a physical safety perspective, this may be the right mind-set if one is not putting himself or herself above others and is merely taking safety measures to ensure a safe environment for one's family. However, if the mind-set is all about protecting me, myself, and I because, "If I do not protect me and mine, I will be doomed," it denotes self-satisfaction, self-will, and self-justification. People with this mind-set are not satisfied unless they are putting this thought into practice. It also denotes self-deception and self-righteousness because to have this mindset is to believe, "If I do not protect myself, my family, and my stuff, I, my family, and my stuff will be unprotected." They strongly believe this thought process is accurate. They are deceiving themselves.

Read Luke 9:57–62. These verses inform us that self-preservation is not the right path. Our lives are not our own. We are not on this earth to protect or save ourselves, our loved ones, or our friends. We are on loan to them, and they are on loan to us, only for as long as God says so. When God calls us, we are to forget about everything and everybody. We are to be totally committed to God, serving only Him. This can only be done by surrendering all, including worldly possessions, and being laser-focused on our assignments.

Life Application

What are your thoughts on this adage: "Self-preservation is the first law of nature"? Explain. Is it biblical? _____

_____

_____

_____

Read the following scriptures.

- Proverbs 12:15
- Proverbs 21:2

- Proverbs 30:12
- 2 Corinthians 10:12
- Lamentations 3:40
- 1 Corinthians 3:13–15

Self-righteousness is the attempt to meet God's standards based on one's own merit. The book of Proverbs has God's instructions regarding living holy. It gives us the pattern by which we, as believers, will obtain wisdom, purity, our work ethic, and moral values. The wisdom of God is often compared and contrasted with the foolishness of the world in the book of Proverbs. To rid ourselves of our selfish ways, we must be willing to read God's Word and apply it in life.

A description of self-righteousness is found in the first three scriptures; they reflect pride issues. Individuals exhibiting these traits have an ignorance of God's Word. They are null and void of understanding the Word of God. In the fourth scripture, Christian believers are instructed to not have the attitude of pride. The last scripture provides a plea that will yield *results*—self-examination. When we read and study God's Word and allow it to reveal to us the depth of our individual depravity and need for a savior, we are conducting a self-examination. It involves searching and reflecting on our innermost thoughts, behaviors, and motivations. If the search reveals a self-mentality and lifestyle, it is time for a change. We cannot protect ourselves, nor can we save ourselves or anyone; that is the business of God. We were permitted to come into this world for a purpose, but not for self-preservation or self-righteousness. All believers will someday stand before the judgment seat of Christ to give an account for our works and service to God. A self-examination is crucial for believers, as our works will be tested. The works will bring either reward or shame when we stand before the Lord.

The *self* mentality denotes self-absorption and self-condemnation. People of this nature are so self-absorbed that they believe it is all about them and that they make things happen. However, when they fail, they tend to blame themselves. Specifically, the self-preservation mind-set is problematic because it destroys faith in the finished work of Jesus at Calvary, for Christ is the savior of the whole world. Therefore, mankind cannot save mankind, nor can mankind save anything, including personal possessions. What is needed is self-examination.

Food for Thought

There is only one who can help us overcome the self-mentality—Jesus Christ, the living Word. The blood of Jesus was provided for us at the cross of Calvary. Let us come to the cross of Jesus and let the blood of Jesus cleanse us from all unrighteousness and selfishness and obtain eternal *results*!

Life Application

Give an example of an attitude of pride. _____
_____
_____
_____

How does pride hamper a Christian's witness? _____
_____
_____
_____

Life Application

Are you willing to totally commit to the Lord? What do you need to do to be totally committed to Him? _____
_____
_____
_____
_____
_____

God's Standard for Christian Living

Jesus Christ established the standard of living for every Christian, and every Christian is called to strive to meet that standard. The standard is multifaceted, entailing several components, including how we should act, react, talk, and walk. Christians must be mindful of what they say and how they say it, and make sure what they say or write does not harm anyone. They must understand that hate speech is not of God; it is evil. It involves verbally and nonverbally expressing extreme dislike for or violence toward a specific person or a group. Hate speech within and of itself is not deemed a crime because it is considered an opinion unless it incites a crime. It is, however, ungodly.

Slander, or making false statements that damage one's reputation, is a crime. Likewise, libel, or writing false statements that damage one's reputation, is a crime. Like slander, gossiping, and spreading rumors, or providing detailed unconfirmed information about someone are not crimes, but the behavior is nowhere near God's standard for Christian living. Thus, Christians must take heed and not permit any of the previously mentioned behaviors work their way into their lives.

In 1 Thessalonians 4:11, Paul advised the Thessalonians to desire to live peacefully, take care of their personal affairs, and not be involved in the affairs of others.

Christians are instructed to help others who are weak, ill, and helpless. It is our Christian duty, but Christians have never been instructed to pry into the lives of others or to repeat what was shared in confidence. Wise Christians know the benefits of not prying or repeating confidential information. This is when we know we are growing in God's grace. More importantly, it is ungodly to engage in such behavior.

Christians are instructed to speak only words that benefit others. When we genuinely love the Lord and become avid readers and doers of His Word, we develop a disciplined lifestyle by refining our speech, which *results* in more gracious and merciful conversations. Careful consideration of what to say and how to say it is wise, as words can lift, and words can hurt (Proverb 18:21). In addition to carefully choosing the right words to say, Christians are instructed to be caring, gentle, and forgiving to others as Christ is to them.

DR. KENNETH HAROLD MCMILLAN

Life Application

How do you measure up to God's standard for living? (Include speech and behaviors.)

_____

_____

_____

_____

Do you attempt to live peaceably with everybody? If so, how? If not, why not?

_____

_____

_____

_____

Read the following scriptures.

- Romans 12:2
- John 13:34
- John 14:15
- John 14:15
- 1 John 4:7
- Philippians 4:7

The Christian walk involves studying and applying the Word of God. Christians are called to a high standard in Christ Jesus—to not adapt to the practices of this world because they are not of God. Christians are called to change their course of thinking from carnal to spiritual. This change in thought would enable Christians to determine what is good and what is evil. When the determination is made, Christians are expected to do what is right—the will of God. Herein lies the high standard expected of Christians.

The Christian walk has eight virtues: new life, faith, spirituality, consistency, love, caution, illumination, and Christlikeness. Born-again Christians are called to walk in the newness of life, which is simply accepting the words of scripture and renouncing our old way of life. It involves becoming more Christlike and praying diligently throughout each day for God to lead and guide.

Traveling through life, Christians do the faith walk. They believe in God and look forward to seeing Him face-to-face. Christians are called to walk in the Spirit. Doing so will keep them from yielding to temptation. Our purpose in life is to make major changes, believing and adhering to the Word of God. Christians are also called out of darkness into the light and are expected to consistently walk in the ways of God. As previously mentioned, Christians are called to walk in love. They are expected to constantly love. They are also expected to be careful in every situation as they walk circumspectly in the light—Jesus. Christians are not only to walk in the light; they are to walk as Christ walked.

The focus of the high standard God has in place for Christians is love. Jesus was the epitome of love. The gospel of John instructs Christians to love one another as Christ loved them. To love God is to be obedient. People observe people, especially those who profess to be Christians, but do not exhibit this most important characteristic. People also observe those who profess to be Christians and express love in action. People will view this expression of love—love in action—as evidence that they are indeed followers of Christ. The world will know that we belong to Christ by the way we love and treat others, which will be our testimony.

Christianity is about doing and not so much about talking. It is one thing to say you love people, but it is another matter to show it. Christians are instructed to show or express love.

Christians should move out of their comfort zone and speak with the Lord. They should ask Him to increase their knowledge of Him and apply His teachings to their heart, mind, and Christian walk. Children of God are called to love. It should come naturally because love comes from God, the Father. Jesus went about doing good, but He was not liked by everyone. In fact, He was hated by many who initially acted as if they loved Him. The same people ended up hating Him to the point of participating in a plot to kill Him.

Like Christ, Christians of today have haters. People smile in their faces and end up doing hateful things to them and murdering with their tongue. Christians are instructed to love in all situations.

As believers, we are called to love our enemies, family, friends, and those who abuse us. It is the very essence of the Christian walk. Oftentimes, however, Christians are on the opposite end of the gossip spectrum. Instead of being a partner in the gossip chain, they find themselves among those being talked about. They hear the negative things others say about them and may be tempted to hate those spreading the gossip. Christians are to take notice of how Jesus responded and follow in His footsteps. He forgave His enemies and never stopped loving and blessing them.

Christians who love try to hurt no one. When we love the way Christ loves, we are well pleasing in His sight. God's standard requires at least three qualities:

Love is one of the qualities, and it is not equal to the others; it is the greatest.

God's standard requires *a repentant heart*, so if at any time love is not exhibited in dealing with others, Christians must show remorse and seek forgiveness. This character trait will ultimately be seen in our dealings with others.

Under God's standard, Christians are instructed to *be the example*. We are called to show and shine the light of Jesus Christ. We must live as model moral citizens who are willing to go above and beyond to glorify Christ. It summons Christians to live a drama-free life, which emanates from God-given peace. That peace—His peace —is incomprehensible and undeniable.

DR. KENNETH HAROLD MCMILLAN

Food for Thought

God's standard for Christians does not include time to be rude, mean, or slanderous toward others. Christians are instructed to be the opposite.

Life Application

How do you walk in faith? _____

_____

_____

_____

How do you walk in the Spirit? _____

_____

_____

_____

How do you walk in love? _____

_____

_____

_____

What is needed to improve your faith walk? Your Spirit walk? Your love walk?

_____

_____

_____

_____

_____

_____

Are you shining the light of Jesus Christ? If so, how? If not, why not? _____

_____

_____

_____

_____

_____

_____

_____

In Galatians 5:22–26, God gives a descriptive definition of the character of believers in Christ and what God produces within them. This is commonly known as the fruit of the spirit. They are character traits that the Lord will grow and develop in us when we follow Him and heed the promptings of the Holy Spirit. How much of the fruit do you see in yourself?

_____

_____

_____

How much of the fruit does God see in you?_____

_____

_____

Which fruit do you have yet to possess? _____

_____

_____

What you do feel you need to do to acquire that fruit? _____

_____

_____

DR. KENNETH HAROLD MCMILLAN

Commitment and Action

To be committed is to be devoted or loyal to a cause or task. John the Baptist was committed to his assigned task to prepare the nation for the Messiah and His arrival. He rebuked sin, called sinners into repentance, and announced God's salvation. He baptized them with water and proclaimed the Messiah would be coming to baptize them with the Holy Spirit. He was fully committed to preaching the gospel, calling people into repentance, telling them what they needed to do. He had holy boldness in proclaiming the gospel truth. However, doing so was costly to him. His commitment cost him his life.

While no one really desires to lose his or her life, Christians must remember that their lives are not their own. John the Baptist was certainly not the only one who had holy boldness. Our Lord and Savior, Jesus Christ, was extremely bold, as He hung, bled, and died on the cross for the sins of all. His desire for all followers was and continues to be that they walk in His shadow and understand that He is their protector. Knowing that God's wrath awaits sinners, Christians should be motivated to share the good news—the Gospel of Jesus Christ—for it is the saving grace for the world.

It is the duty of every Christian to share the gospel of Jesus Christ with the unsaved. God demands results from every believer. If people are to grasp eternal life, they must hear about eternal judgment. Christians must be found faithful in ministry in preparing the hearts of the people and presenting Christ to them. One plants and one waters, and God gives the increase. The goal of Christians should be *one* soul at a time. John the Baptist faithfully completed his God-given assignment and prepared others to meet Jesus. Christians should be ready to tell others the truth of the Gospel.

Food for Thought

A committed life is a life of dedication and service.

Life Application

Are you committed to the cause of Christ? Explain._____
_____
_____
_____
_____

Your life is not your own. Explain. _____
_____
_____
_____
_____

DR. KENNETH HAROLD MCMILLAN

Mind-Set

Read James 1:1–12

Dealing with difficult people or difficult situations can be difficult within itself. However, our perceptions of the difficulties can be helpful or hurtful, positive, or negative. The people to whom James wrote in the first 12 verses of chapter 1 had endured difficult times in persecution. James asked them to reflect on their views concerning adverse encounters. He advised them to be positive when being tested and presented the scripture. We all experience difficult circumstances, but the key is to learn how to trust God in the process. Some difficult circumstances in life include death, divorce, disappointments, and despair.

When death takes our loved ones and friends, we must trust God for strength to make it through. Divorce is like a death; suddenly, the couple is no longer a couple, as one has departed. Trusting in God is a must during this critical period, as He is needed as a guide through the loneliness, aloneness, anger, and bitterness that accompany death and divorce. Disappointments are also a part of life, but in the flesh, we are not equipped within ourselves to deal with them. We must trust God to comfort and guide us. Additionally, some situations cause us to be in despair, to feel hopeless. When in this mode, we must trust God to pull us out of the misery.

God knew we would be confronted with the issues previously described because He gave us a Word on all of them. Regarding death, His Word comforts us. This scripture applies to divorce as well because of the pain experienced in the process. Regarding disappointments, there are times when we wonder why. In hopelessness, we can rest in the Word. Thus, tough times and heartaches can be quite difficult. However, these times place us in a teaching-learning position. This position is considered the university of hard knocks. It is in this place that we observe God working a work in us, renewing our mind, preparing us to move forward, and equipping us for the next level.

Food for Thought

Difficulties are a part of life.

Life Application

How do you deal with difficulties? (Include difficult people and circumstances.) _____

_____

_____

_____

_____

DR. KENNETH HAROLD MCMILLAN

Watering, Working, and Warning

CHRISTIANS MUST NEVER accept spiritual immaturity as normal or acceptable because it is not. In the physical realm, something is wrong if one never matures because the cycle of life exists. Maturing is a process of developing or evolving. Babies evolve into toddlers, and toddlers evolve into preschool children. Preschool children evolve into middle school children, and middle school children evolve into adolescents. The next stage is adulthood, or age nineteen. However, brain-development scientists have determined that true maturity is not reached until age twenty-five (*Mental Health Daily*, 2013–19).

Babies are fed baby food. As they grow older, when their stomachs can digest it, they are fed solid food. The same is applicable to the spiritual life. Born-again Christians must be taught the basics of Christianity in increments. Care should be taken to not provide them with advanced biblical teachings before they have digested the basics.

Nothing should be assumed. As new converts grow in the Word, they are introduced to more advanced biblical principles, and the cycle goes on. Once they reach a degree of maturity, they are expected to act as they have been taught. Their lives should reflect their teachings. In the developmental stages of life, some do not mature, or at least they do not act as if they have matured when they reach age twenty-five. The same, however, applies with some born-again Christians. They do not act as though they have matured to any degree. Some act as if they are baby Christians, still needing milk.

In conversing with the members of the church at Corinth, Paul was apparently disheartened by the behavior of the Corinthians. He had taught them biblical principles and discovered they had reverted to carnal behavior and regressed into spiritual infancy—some had gone back to acting like spoiled babies, living carnally and not spiritually. This childish behavior on the part of the believers in the church at Corinth represented a poor testimony to the unbelievers in their local community.

Life Application

Where are you on the spiritual growth ladder? (A babe in Christ? A maturing Christian?) Explain.

_____

_____

_____

Read the following scriptures.

- 1 Corinthians 3:1–3
- Proverbs 27:6

In Paul's eyes, members of the church at Corinth should have been beyond milk and ready for solid food. However, that was not the case. Envy and jealousy were causing division. They were acting like non-Christians, like people of the world and not like people of God. They brought worldliness into the church, causing disharmony. There is, however, no place for division or disharmony in the church. Christians must have a desire to grow, change, and get in alignment with God's Word. Otherwise, they will remain baby Christians, not fulfilling the purpose for which they came into this world.

Paul had to reprimand members of the Corinthian church for their unholy behavior and remind them that their carnal conduct would not result in spiritual rewards. Paul's words of correction inflicted much pain on the believers, but he knew that in the long run, they would benefit spiritually. Paul approached the members of the church at Corinth as true friends. True friends willingly confront their brothers and sisters about their ungodly ways. Paul's attitude changed from one of vigorous chastening to defending his strong words of correction. He reminded them that he and the other apostles came as servants of Christ and stewards of the mysteries of God to bring them hope of salvation by sharing the good news of grace. Only those who are true to the call would risk damaging valuable friendships by addressing errors of judgment in efforts to encourage correction of faults.

Paul taught the members of the church at Corinth the truth of the gospel of grace. He pleaded and prayed on behalf of others. He stood up for the righteousness of Christ. There is no greater virtue than that of the love of God and others. It is what God requires of Christians. The characteristics that the natural man so values are intellect, wealth, position, power, and success. However, faithfulness and loyalty to God and the church are the attributes He seeks in His servants.

Food for Thought

Holiness and worldliness do not mix.

Life Application

Are you faithful and loyal to God? Explain. If not, what do you need to do to become faithful and loyal to Him? _____

_____

_____

_____

Are you faithful and loyal to the church? Explain. If not, what do you need to do to become faithful and loyal to the church? _____

_____

_____

_____

Being transparently open and honest with God and the church is paramount. All Christians are called to be faithful in fulfilling all duties. Faithfulness is an important criterion for servants and stewards of God. They are required to be trustworthy and faithful. Paul wanted the members of the church at Corinth to understand that challenging their carnal behavior and chastening their ungodly ways was proof that Paul was trustworthy and a true steward of the gospel. He was not only faithful to God but to the entire Corinthian church.

Paul noted that Christians are fellow laborers working in the vineyard. Some are called to plant the seed and others to water it. They work as one, being used by God to fulfill His purpose. Ministry leaders can only sow and water the spiritual seed. Christians are to serve God diligently with their gifts and give God the glory for all success. Paul noted that the Lord alone causes growth (1 Corinthians 3:5–7).

Life Application

What are you contributing to the growth of the church?

_____

_____

_____

What are you contributing to the growth of people?

_____

_____

_____

What are you contributing to the growth of the community?

_____

_____

_____

What are you contributing to the growth of ministry?

_____

_____

_____

Read the following scriptures.

- Ephesians 2:20–21
- Corinthians 3:11
- Romans 14:12
- Daniel 12:3
- John 9:4
- Matthew 25:23
- Deuteronomy 15:15
- 2 Peter 3:9
- Romans 12:9

Unity and cooperation are a must. All Christians are to build upon the foundation of the church, Jesus Christ, as He is the chief cornerstone. Jesus is the only intercessor, the only remedy, the only nourishment, the only source of truth, and the only savior. He is the only foundation.

Some Christians will receive a spiritual reward because of their faithfulness. All Christians should be about doing God's will, finishing divine tasks, completing the course joyfully, attaining Christlikeness, working as Jesus worked. We must be diligent in accomplishing our mission and reminded of the brevity of life. Jesus was cognizant of his limited time on the earth, and He did not waste it. Faithfulness yields _results_.

The Bible is the Christians' blueprint for life. Instructions are outlined as to what to do and what not to do. God, the creator of life, gave us a conscious. His Word tells us He gave us options—to choose life or death. God does not force anyone to do anything. We are to make the choice. If we choose good, we will live; if we choose evil, we will die. It is, however, not His will that we should die. He never forces Himself on anybody, but it is His desire that we choose what is good, righteous, and fair, and that we despise wickedness.

Read the following scriptures.

- Isaiah 5:20–21
- 1 Corinthians 15:33
- Proverbs 3:7
- Psalm 37:2

God did not promise that we would simply exist if we choose good. He promised great blessings if we love Him, follow Him, and remain obedient to His Word. As aforementioned, if we choose evil, God's Word tells us that it will not be for our good. The Word of God expressly warns against having evil relations or interactions. It instructs us in Proverbs and Psalms to remove ourselves from evil.

Mutual Love

Read the following scriptures.

- Ecclesiastes 4:12
- 1 John 3:14

Mutual love is the product and command of Christ. Upon Christ's departure from earth, He made provisions for His work to be perpetual among His people (believers). Love is the unifying cords that strengthen His body of believers. You, plus me, plus Christ, equal a love bond. Faith in Christ, love to one another, and benevolent work in Jesus's name are the three facets of Christian discipleship and the three elements by which the church was to be cemented into true unity.

Mutual love is promised, motivated, and modeled by Christ (love for His people). To the Christian, Jesus is the master in *all* conduct, the spiritual power that accounts for the renewed character in all phases of life. We show devotion to Christ by loving people the way that He loved them. The model—Christ alone—is the perfect example. The love of Jesus Christ is active, practical, and self-sacrificing. Avoid the path of least resistance: I don't, I won't, I can't, and I quit.

Mutual love is proof of Christian discipleship. Anyone who does not love remains in death. Love is the badge of Jesus Christ. The life of grace in the heart of a regenerated person is the beginning and first principle of a life of glory. However, those who hate their brothers in their hearts will be destitute. Christians should check themselves before they wreck themselves. If there is no pain, there will be no gain as sacrifices must be made. Dying to self and old ways is mandatory. Mutual love is the profound effect of Christ in our life.

The attributes of mutual love are outlined here with the accompanying biblical reference.

- Love one another (John 13:35);
- Admonish (warn) one another (Romans 15:14);
- Serve one another (Galatians 5:13);
- Bear one another's burden (Galatians 6:2);
- Be kind to one another (Ephesians 4:32);
- Be subject to one another (Ephesians 5:21);
- Comfort one another (1 Thessalonians 4:18);

DR. KENNETH HAROLD MCMILLAN

- Live in peace with one another (1 Thessalonians 5:13);
- Confess sins to one another (James 5:16); and
- Be hospitable to one another (1 Peter 4:9).

Our Lord Jesus Christ is the epitome of mutual love. We should have no problem being mutually in love with Him. In loving Him, we must truly allow His mind—with all its selflessness, humility, patience, kindness, goodness, and self-control—to shape our lives.

Are you in a mutual love relationship with God? Explain. If not, how can you enter into a mutual love relationship with God? _____
_____
_____
_____

Food for Thought

Move toward a life rooted in mutual love for mankind.

Promise of a New Covenant

Read the following scriptures.

- Deuteronomy 6:4–9
- Matthew 5:43–48

In the Old Testament, God wrote the covenant on tablets. In the New Testament, God wrote the covenant on the heart of His people. The old covenant was written on stone and the people were to internalize the laws. The plan was that the new covenant would be written on our hearts by God, founded upon the concept of the life, death, burial, resurrection, and the second coming of our Lord Jesus Christ, the Gospel of Jesus. The Gospel of Jesus Christ came to all who would believe that God had provided a way for man to renew and restore his relationship with God. The problem was that mankind had drifted so far away from God. Jesus knew that the only way man could enjoy an intimate and personal relationship back with God was by Him building or becoming the bridge that would lead us back to God.

The major problem was that people had become so rebellious in their thoughts, minds, and actions that it pushed them away from God. They had knowledge in their heads but no love for God in their hearts. Jeremiah had to encourage the nation of Israel to surrender to Babylon because the Babylonians were the chosen people and the instrument that God used to judge the nation's sins. God used a pagan nation to prayerfully turn His people back to Him. He is sovereign and holy. He can use whomever or whatever—an individual, a group of people, animals, or instruments—to speak life into His people. The nation knew what God required; they simply did as they pleased. The people of God had failed to keep God's laws, and He was not pleased. Therefore, He judged them. Because of head knowledge and no heart knowledge, God promised to put the law inside them. He wrote it on their hearts. He eventually sent the Holy Spirit to advocate for mankind.

Food for Thought

- When God uses the word "behold," it means pay attention. At times it is a prediction of God's wrath and punishment.

DR. KENNETH HAROLD MCMILLAN

- God does not punish innocent people. Innocent people, at times, get caught up in the collateral damage of others.
- Some believers blame their distressing circumstances on others. Taking responsibility for one's own actions and consequences are paramount for growth and development.
- The church is the body of believers. It is corporate.

Questions

God holds two entities accountable—corporate and personal—the church and the individual believer. For what does God hold each accountable? Explain.

a. Corporate _____

_____

_____

b. Personal _____

_____

_____

Does God require head knowledge or heart knowledge? Explain. _____

_____

_____

_____

In Jeremiah 31:31, God makes a promise about the last days in Jeremiah 31:31. What is the promise? _____

_____

_____

Read Hebrews 8:8–12. What is the new covenant to which God refers in Verse 10?

_____

_____

_____

In Verse 12, what specifically did God promise the house of Israel regarding their sins?

_____

_____

_____

God's Covenant with Abram

A COVENANT IS AN agreement. The biblical covenant is an agreement between God and His people. Several covenants were made between God and His people in the Old Testament.

The first was the covenant in this lesson, between God and Abraham. God promised Abraham that his descendants would be afflicted for a period but would be victorious and inherit the land. God stated that he would be merciful and not only forgive the sins of mankind; he would also forget them. If we believe in Jesus Christ, the Son of God, God will grant us everlasting life. Thus, faith is a major component in the new covenant. Promise of everlasting life.

Read the scriptures noted below and answer the corresponding questions in your own words, explain.

In Genesis 15:1, God speaks. To whom did God speak? _____
_____
_____

How did God convey His message? _____
_____
_____

What was God's message? _____
_____
_____

In Genesis 15:2–3, What was the response of the person to whom God spoke? _____
_____
_____

In Genesis 15:4–5, God pronounced His blessing. What did God say? _____
_____
_____

DR. KENNETH HAROLD MCMILLAN

What did God do? _____

_____

_____

What was the pronouncement? _____

_____

_____

In Genesis 15:6, Abram believes. This statement is significant because Paul referenced it several times in the book of Romans (4:3, 4:9, and 4:22) and at least once in Galatians 3:6. James also referenced it in James 2:23. Why do you feel it was so significant to Paul and James? _____

_____

_____

Do you feel it is significant for Christians today? If so, why? If not, why not? _____

_____

_____

In Genesis 15:7–11, Gods reveals His plan for Abram and provides instructions.

What question did Abram pose to God? _____

_____

_____

Is he denying his blessings by asking this question? Explain your response. _____

_____

_____

Is faith at work here? Explain. _____

_____

_____

What did God instruct Abram to do? _____

_____

_____

God sealed the deal with Abraham in the shedding of the animals' blood and body pieces. In Abram's sleep, God passed through the pieces of the dead animals alone. Nothing depended on Abraham. Everything depended on God. Abraham and his seed could trust and believe that God was faithful to everything that He promised. All God's promises are fulfilled in Jesus.

Life Application

How does faith grow and enhance our daily walk with the Lord? _____
_____
_____

How would you encourage fellow believers to have faith in the most difficult circumstances?
_____
_____

What personal responsibilities have the Lord placed upon your heart? _____
_____
_____

When we, as believers, trust the whole counsel of God, how far can He really take us? (Refer to and cite scriptural reference for God's actual words.) _____
_____
_____

What prevents believers from fully and wholeheartedly trusting God at His Word? _____
_____
_____

How can we trust God and follow Jesus with an even deeper walk? _____
_____
_____

Read 1 Corinthians 9:16. What has God called you to do in this life? _____
_____
_____

Life Application

The word woe means calamity or trouble. What does God require of you so you will not be or endure a calamity? Fill in the blank ___ **b**__ __ __ __ __ **c**__

DR. KENNETH HAROLD MCMILLAN

Loyalty to Leaders

Being loyal means being faithful, devoted, and reliable. The Word of God stresses that Christians should be loyal to the leaders assigned to them. Jesus was the most loyal servant while serving on this earth and remains in first place today. While He was a servant, He was and still reigns as the King of kings and Lord of lords.

Life Application

Read Hebrews 13:17. Do you accept the God-given authority of your pastor? If so, why? How?

_____

_____

_____

Do you believe that the scriptures tell us that Jesus is head of the church and that Christ has appointed all leadership in the church and in the world? If so, on what scripture are you basing your response? _____

_____

_____

_____

Obedience

Read Hebrews 13:17

Obedience is when we submit ourselves to a God-given command. It is wholeheartedly believing what God said and doing what He said because He said it. It requires action and movement. It also requires submission, responsibility, and accountability.

Submission is the act of placing oneself under the authority of another. In Matthew 6, Jesus teaches about submission in the model prayer, often called the Lord's Prayer. It is surrendering our will over to God and following His will.

Responsibility is when we take ownership in the Lord. It is when we hold to a high standard when being compelled to complete our assignments for the Lord Jesus.

Accountability is the act of being obligated to do something, or do something one is expected to do. We are accountable to God because we are expected to live out the Word of God. We are also expected to faithfully complete our assignments on the job, in the church, or wherever we are assigned. But more importantly, we are expected to complete our God-given assignments.

Food for Thought

- We must not have a halfhearted approach. We must be all in. Partial obedience is disobedience.
- The Lord desires our whole heart. When we read the Bible or when the scriptures are taught, we must be extremely careful to obey all that the Lord has said and given to us.
- If we want to have God's blessings in our lives, we must be willing to hear and do God's will.
- We must be willing to obey God and not people, friends, or the local norms.

DR. KENNETH HAROLD MCMILLAN

Life Application

Do you believe that you are a good follower? Explain. _____
_____
_____
_____

What attributes do you need to be a good or an improved servant for our Lord Jesus Christ?
_____
_____
_____

Are you willing to ask the Lord to make you one of His faithful followers? If so, what are you willing to do to become a faithful follower? _____
_____
_____
_____

Perseverance

Perseverance may be defined as enduring, regardless of the time factor, holding out until the end. Jesus, the Son of God, is, was, and will forever be the world's absolute perfect model of perseverance and leadership. Paul was a strong man of God and great leader who endured many sufferings for the cause of Christ. Several other characters in biblical history also persevered. Joseph, Moses, and Job were among them.

Review the following scriptures.

- Genesis 37:23–28
- Genesis 39:6–20
- Exodus 5–14
- Job 1–42

Joseph was thrown into a well, sold into slavery by his brothers, and placed in captivity for more than a decade by Potiphar. He continued being faithful to God and received *results*—blessings from God! Moses endured much under Pharaoh, remained faithful to God, followed God's instructions, and he and the Israelites received *results*—miraculous freedom! Job endured numerous tragedies and hardships, personal and business, but he remained faithful to God and received *results*—blessings galore, more than he had before, including long life!

Food for Thought

Blessings are tied to perseverance in the service of the Lord.

Life Application

Are you willing to endure hardships while serving God? Explain. (Consider faithfulness and time.)

_____

_____

Education, Entertainment, and Entitlement

Read Proverbs 7:1–5.

I. Son of Man (Son of God): Jesus versus Joker, Spiderman, and Black Panther

    A. Reality versus fantasy: video games, recreation ball

    B. -. Be realistic; fewer than 0.50 percent of athletes go professional (education, entertainment, or entitlement).

II. Love versus hate: choose love. It covers a multitude of sins; it never fails.

    A. Word of God versus worldly wisdom—no more "blame game."

    B. Godly versus worldly: see Romans 12:1–2. Education, Christian duty in a surrendered life. There must be total submission to the Lord.

III. Needs versus wants: needs are defined as goods or services that are required. This includes clothing, shelter, food, and health-care. Teach the value of needs versus wants.

    A. Wants are goods that we desire.

    B. We need clothes, but we do not need name brands or designer clothes.

IV. Transportation: Riding the bus versus driving a car. How important is it to reach your destination? No one is entitled to anything!

V. Perception versus reality: teach your children the value of having godly integrity.

    A. Children falsely believe the world is going to do for them what you went overboard and did.

    B. Educate/teach work ethic, hard work, sacrifice, and knowing God's will.

Life Application

Compare TV and the Bible. _____
_____
_____
_____

Compare love versus hate. _____
_____
_____
_____

Compare needs versus wants. _____
_____
_____
_____

How do you see your life in comparison to these concepts? _____
_____
_____
_____

Integrity is doing the right thing, regardless of your situation or consequences. Cite an example of a situation that revealed you had integrity. _____
_____
_____
_____

Read Isaiah 5:20–21 (good versus evil). Explain what the prophet Isaiah is communicating in these two verses. Cite examples. _____
_____
_____
_____

Read John 3:30. What does this scripture indicate you must do? What happens as a result of doing what the scripture instructs? _____
_____
_____
_____

DR. KENNETH HAROLD MCMILLAN

Read Psalm 37:16. Explain the principle established in this scripture. _____

_____

_____

_____

We obtain, find, or gain by losing. When we die to ourselves, we glorify God, and His will becomes our will. The Bible is clear that gaining Jesus is the best thing that can happen to us.

Read Galatians 2:20. Explain the statement: "We live by dying." _____

_____

_____

_____

Read Matthew 23:12. According to this scripture, what is the consequence of exalting oneself? What is the blessing for being humble? _____

_____

_____

_____

Choices—Decisions

Trust God and follow Jesus. Throughout scripture, the Lord informs us that faith and obedience must work together. We must study the inerrant Word of God and do what He says, without any doubt.

Life Application

What does it mean to have an intimate relationship with Jesus? _____

_____

_____

_____

Explain the statement "Jesus is my Lord and Savior." _____

_____

_____

_____

How committed are you to following Jesus? Explain your commitment. _____

_____

_____

_____

Does personal obedience draw others to Christ? Explain. _____

_____

_____

_____

DR. KENNETH HAROLD MCMILLAN

I Am Who You Say I Am

Knowing God involves having a real relationship with Him. It also involves intimately knowing His son, Jesus. Additionally, it involves permitting Him to be Savior and Lord.

Life Application

Who is Jesus to you? Explain. _____
_____
_____
_____

Where is Jesus in your life? Is He still outside? Explain. _____
_____
_____
_____

Why is Jesus where He is with you? _____
_____
_____
_____

Cite something you have done with Jesus. _____
_____
_____
_____

Jesus, the Son of God, is referenced in several ways. Explain why you believe He is referenced as indicated below.

Prince of Peace _____
_____
_____

Wonderful Counselor _____
_____
_____

Mighty God _____
_____
_____

Everlasting Father _____
_____
_____

Are you ready and willing to give an honest testimony regarding who Jesus is to you? If so, what would you include? _____
_____
_____

DR. KENNETH HAROLD MCMILLAN

Properly Planning, Pressing, Praying, and Progressing

Read Philippians 3:12–14.

1. Attitude adjustment—attaining Christlikeness (the Mind of Christ).

   A. Philippians 2:5–11, the Humble and Exalted Christ;
   B. Romans 12:1–2, Christian duty to a surrendered life;
   C. Fight fear faithfully—understand Calvary's cross

2. Bankable belief is trusting God at His Word; believing all of the promises of God are true. Yes and amen.

3. Christlike consistency is accepting responsibility; no more blaming others for your shortfalls; no more lying. No excuses.

   A. Luke 9:23–26
   B. Fight fear faithfully—Calvary's cross
   C. Have an attitude of gratification

4. Determine disciples of your made-up mind. Turn the TV off. Turn your phone off. Ignore social media. Do God's will.

   A. Make a determined decision to follow Jesus;
   B. Fight fear faithfully—Calvary's cross
   C. No more excuses

5. Enhance education by studying more; develop quiet time. Go deeper with more reading of the Word.

   A. 2 Timothy 2:15;
   B. Education or entertainment. Playing or Praying. Emphasize ethics early;

C. Fight fear faithfully—Calvary's cross;

D. We must remember to always take it to Jesus in prayer.

6. Financially frugal—your emergency fund should be $1,000 minimum. Place a focus on making sacrifices. Save for short- and long-term goals. Invest in your future. Be ready to share when the Lord says so.

   A. Acts 20:35;

   B. The rich will always have the advantage over the poor in this world;

   C. Fight fear faithfully—Calvary's cross;

   D. Give your finances over to saturated prayer.

7. Godly goal (setups): Find out God's will and purpose for your life. Eat less. Pray more. Read to expand your mind. Don't allow social media to dictate your life and days. Set true attainable goals.

   A. Philippians 3:12–14;

   B. Fight fear faithfully—Calvary's cross;

   C. Be more determined to be a point of light for Jesus Christ.

I invite you today to meet me at the cross. Jesus is waiting. All are welcome.

DR. KENNETH HAROLD MCMILLAN

Your Financial Emergency Kit

Gᴏᴅ ʜᴀs ᴀ perfect plan in place for His people (Jeremiah 29.1). We must, however, use wisdom and understanding in following His dictates. We must also have the positive mind-set that we will be successful.

I. Set priorities. Tithe and honor God *before* anything and everything. Your "field" is not just something you need for survival. It is actually a means of survival.

    A. What good is a house if you do not have the means to put food on the table or to pay the rent/mortgage?

    B. Set priorities with your money. Have enough to cover your essentials.

    C. Set aside money to pay the bills before you spend any on new clothes or luxuries.

II. Create a budget for yourself and your family

    A. Cover the cost of necessities first, and do this as often as you can. Plan for expenses or make a budget.

    B. Physically write out the bills and expenses, weekly grocery list, utility bills, and retirement savings.

III. Create an emergency/rainy-day fund because you will need it one day.

    A. Think about unforeseen emergency events that may occur.

    B. Do you have enough set aside in an emergency fund for living expenses for at least six months if needed?

    C. During the lean and overflow years, be frugal. Take extreme care with money. Be prepared for unplanned and unforeseen shortages.

IV. Avoid debt

    A. Proverbs 22:7 notes that the rich rule over the poor and the borrower is a slave to the lender.

    B. Debt is associated with anxiety, depression, anger, relationship problems, high blood pressure, lower immunity, headaches, back pain, and ulcers.

V. Diversify your investments

    A. Ecclesiastes 11:2 says to invest in seven or eight ventures. You do not know what disaster may come upon the land.

    B. Put your money into different investments so a single disaster will not be devastatingly costly.

    C. The more you diversify, the more you reduce your risk. The younger you are, the more risk you can take. The older you become, the safer you want to invest.

VI. Reduce the risk as you age. Move from up-and-down stocks to slow-growth but dependable bonds.

    A. The father who loses everything on a bad investment and leaves no legacy is an awful testimony.

    B. Leave an inheritance for your true loved ones.

    C. Leave high-risk investments (stocks) and enter in lower-risk investments (bonds, annuities) that will give you a modest income (such as a Roth IRA).

VII. Create a financial plan.

    A. Plan A to Z for your finances.

    B. Do not make rash and foolish money decisions. Get an accountability prayer partner.

    C. Rashness is acting without forethought or due caution. Think before you recklessly spend.

Food for Thought

- Identify your goals. Write personal goals and visit them often.
- Evaluate your situation. Determine your own personal net worth. Find out how much you are earning and how much you are spending, and what kinds of returns are your currently getting on your investments. Get a vision but more importantly, get an action plan for life.

- List steps to take and determine your end game. Ask yourself: From where do I start? When do I start?
- Remember to trust God and follow Jesus.

Wisdom is needed to live a life for Christ. Godly wisdom will help us become motivated to do His will and maintain our financial emergency kit. Trust God and His wisdom, which is only found in the Holy scriptures. It is the Word of God that will yield *results*.

Do Not Spend What You Do Not Have!

Read the following scriptures.

- Matthew 6:24
- Luke 2:8–13

I. Half-heartedness and doublemindedness are one and the same, and it causes tremendous debt and trouble.

    A. Being doubleminded causes one to be unbalanced in all endeavors (James 1:8).

    B. One heart cannot serve two masters. Choices must be made. Spend and save God's way, or spend now and pay later. (Check your credit score and view your debt-to-credit ratio: low or high, good or bad? Ask: "Is this something that is a need (must-have), or is it a want?"

    C. A life is either all spiritual or not spiritual at all. It is all about choices and decision making. In Matthew 4, Jesus is tempted by Satan to do something stupid.

Either you serve

- Jesus or Satan;
- The world or the Word;
- Flesh or the spirit;
- Righteousness or unrighteousness; or
- Good or evil.

We must be willing to surrender our lives to become the people the Lord desires and allow God to use us for His will and purpose.

II. The allurement (power, temporary prosperity) of sin

    A. determines the fate of the wicked and disobedient. Debt and slow payments equal higher notes, more interest, and longer payments (Proverbs 22:7).

DR. KENNETH HAROLD MCMILLAN

B. leads to earthly honor and earthly reward. It also leads to temptation to do and have the latest gifts and gadgets and to not honor God with your God-given gifts, talents, time, or treasures.

Food for Thought

Debt is easy to get into and hard to get out of. Do not spend what you do not have.

Read 2 Corinthians 5:10. In what are you investing your life? Earthly or eternal gains? _____

_____

_____

God invested in us by sending His Son, Jesus. He was not earthly rich. He came and was wrapped in swaddling clothes. He died and was buried in a borrowed tomb. The message is that we should invest in people, not things and materials, but in the lives and souls of God's people.

III. No more being neutral. Neutrality is not possible in spiritual things. Remember, make a concerted decision to be biblically wise in your spending and saving.

A. The Bible tells us to make wise godly decisions and to seek godly counsel when we are unsure.
B. An honest desire to do right preserves a man from fatal mistakes. Some who are extremely poor trade and spend as if they were rich: This is sin, and it is shameful.

How much money did God spend on Jesus?

- No money down. He left us with sin debt paid in full.
- No layaway plans—no pay some down and pay some later. (The perfect plan.)
- No credit card—buy now and pay later.

God spent His heart on Jesus!

Life Application

What are you willing to spend on the lost? _____

_____

_____

Financial Freedom

Established priorities reveal your character. Do not trust in riches (money), but trust in He who richly provides and supplies all needs. Your heart is where your treasure is located. Make sure your treasure is in the place that will grant you financial freedom.

Read Proverbs 3:9–10: the path to financial freedom is found in these verses.

Life Application

What is the instruction in Verse 9? _____
_____
_____

In your own words, state the promise noted in Verse 10 for following the instruction in Verse 9.
_____
_____

Read Proverbs 6:6–11. What principle is noted in these verses that will assist one in solving financial problems? _____
_____
_____

I. Financial problems cannot be resolved by doing the following:

    A. Competing with/comparing what you have with what others have.

    B. Frequenting the clearance section or the on-sale, everything-must-go sections!

    C. Not differentiating between *wants* and *needs*.

II. Financial freedom tips.

    A. Pay with cash only.

B. Limit the use of debit and credit cards.

C. Plan for

    a. emergencies

    b. retirement

    c. children's futures

Apply Proverbs 3:9.

Food for Thought

Read Proverbs 23:12

- You cannot ask God to make room for you in heaven if you have no room for Jesus (the Word) in your heart.
- God gives us wealth so that He can establish His covenant.
- Apply your ears to the words of knowledge and understand the purpose of money.
- Base all decisions on biblical wisdom.
- Knowledge of the purpose for money and careful financial planning are lifelong skills to help you remain financially strong year after year.
- Read Matthew 16:26.
- Don't give in to the love of this world and lose your very soul.

Burning Bridges

Aʟʟ ᴀssᴇssᴍᴇɴᴛs ᴏꜰ what is good should be guided by the parameters established by God's Word. Deception is trickery. It comes in the form of misguiding people. An example is rephrasing or wrongly dividing the Word of God. Satan is and has been a deceiver since the beginning (John 8:44). He draws people into sin.

Read and compare Genesis 3:2–3 and Genesis 2:15–17. Share your thoughts. _____

_____

_____

_____

Temptation involves being allured toward sin, trials, and difficulties of believers. Eve saw the "good" of eating the fruit. She knew that it was useful for food, and it was practical and beautiful. Satan questioned whether eating the forbidden fruit was a sin.

Read 1 John 2:16. What are the three categories of temptation outlined in this scripture? _____

_____

_____

_____

Doubt leads to denials, which is a dangerous place to be. It also leads to consistently making bad decisions, which oftentimes leads to lying. Additionally, it leads to questioning what God really said. It can come in the form of a question such as, "Are you certain?"

Read Matthew 17:17. What did Jesus do in this scripture? _____

_____

_____

_____

　　　　DR. KENNETH HAROLD MCMILLAN

Have you ever doubted something God told you to do? Explain. _____

_____

_____

_____

Disobedience is the failure or refusal to obey rules or someone in authority. It is knowing God's will and refusing to do it.

Food for Thought

- Audit the sin.
- Ask God for forgiveness.
- Receive His blessings.
- Obey God's call.
- Accept the miracle of the cross. Choose Jesus and obtain *results*!

Do Not Believe the Hype

THE DEVIL IS a distinct fact. He is well-defined in the Bible. We lived with him when we were lost in darkness, but God saved and sanctified us. We are in the light and must be determined to live as children of the light (Ephesians 5:8–9). We must tell others that the devil is not a fairy tale about ghosts, goblins, candy, and costumes. He is on a mission to deceive and trick us to not follow Jesus.

The devil is a determined force. He is on a mission to take as many souls to hell with him and his fallen angels. Do not follow Satan, Halloween, or the world. Do not participate with the devil on his day and lose your Christian witness. Pray for others to be safe, saved, and secured with Jesus. Tell others that this day is about honoring the devil. Be sure to tell them about Jesus (John 10:10).

The devil is a defeated foe. He is not your friend. Halloween is not innocent. It does major spiritual damage in the world. It is shameful even to mention what the disobedient do in secret, but everything exposed by the light becomes visible, and everything that is illuminated becomes a light. Share your faith about Jesus with others. Satan will win some battles, but he must not take your soul with him. Fight for others and tell them about the lovingkindness of Jesus. Do not lose your soul by following the devil. Choose Jesus and His righteousness and obtain *results*.

Food for Thought

Take a stand for Jesus and find out what pleases Him (Ephesians 5:11).

Life Application

How can you share your faith about Jesus on Halloween? _____

_____

_____

DR. KENNETH HAROLD MCMILLAN

Spiritual Warfare

Spiritual warfare involves wrestling or fighting with evil or oppositional forces. Christians are constantly engaged in spiritual warfare and are strongly advised to be prepared. The state of mind is extremely important in dealing with spiritual warfare. This is especially true for Christians. The spiritual and the carnal are always in a battle. The situation or circumstance does not matter; however, one will win over the other every time. The victor will be the one we feed the most. If we feed the spiritual self, it will override the carnal. On the contrary, if we feed the carnal, it will override the spiritual. These two forces are in battle within our minds.

The carnal is not of God. Paul described his battle in Romans 7:21. At the time of his struggles, Paul expressed that he did the opposite of what he desired to do. He desired to do what was right, but he found himself doing what was wrong. He realized, though, that his old nature, the flesh, was crucified with Christ. Sin was taken care of at the cross. Once converted, Paul stayed true to the faith. He remained committed to his God-given assignment. Referencing his impending death and reflecting on his new life in Christ, Paul alluded to the *results*. He noted that he had completed his God-given assignment and had been faithful throughout the journey. He knew he had served well. He overcame the battle with the flesh and became a slave to our Lord and Savior. Most importantly, he was prepared to meet his Creator. The Word of God instructs us on how to prepare for spiritual warfare.

Food for Thought

Feed the good spirit. When the carnal ascends, cast it down.

Read 1 Peter 5:8. What is happening before spiritual warfare begins? _____

_____

_____

What are you instructed to do at this time? _____

_____

_____

How do you deal with spiritual warfare? _____

_____

_____

Read Ephesians 6:10–17. What are Christians instructed to do in this scripture? _____

_____

_____

Why must Christians adhere to the instructions? _____

_____

_____

What itemized list is presented in these scriptures? _____

_____

_____

Read 2 Corinthians 10:4–5. What is the good news about the spiritual weapons? _____

_____

_____

Read James 4:7. What are Christians instructed to do to be successful in spiritual warfare? ____

_____

_____

Read Isaiah 54:17. What consolation do Christians have while in spiritual warfare? _____

_____

_____

Life Application

Read 2 Timothy 4:7. Have you started your race for Jesus? Explain. _____

_____

_____

DR. KENNETH HAROLD MCMILLAN

Are you fighting for your loved ones to receive the good news of Jesus? Explain. _____

_____

_____

If not, explain. _____

_____

_____

Are you going above and beyond for family members, coworkers, and friends to learn about Jesus? Explain. _____

_____

_____

Baptism Is a Love Thing

GOD IS LOVE (1 John 4:7–8). John challenges believers in the church to love one another because love comes from God. Baptism is an outward sign of the love of Christ. When we love others, we express the very heart of God. This is compassionate love. Loving God is a sign that we are born of God with renewed hearts. Love is the mark of a relationship between God and man, which yields great *results*!

The supreme example of love is illustrated in 1 John 4:9–12. God showed genuine love for us when He sent His only son to die on the cross for our sins. The justice of God had to be met, and we had to be forgiven, so He sent Jesus to stand in our place of condemnation so that we could be set free. Thus, we have reason to show the world our love for Jesus. God sent the one closest to His heart to die for us, despite our sins, to show us that we are close to His heart. Jesus was the sacrifice for our sins. Baptism symbolizes our belief and acceptance.

The proof of God's love for us is outlined in 1 John 4:13–16. God sent His Holy Spirit to live within us to give us the power to love those we cannot love in our own sinful nature. The Holy Spirit lives in us and reminds us that He empowers us to love. Those who have Jesus living in their hearts and lives will, without hesitation, proclaim the truth that Jesus is the savior of the world. Baptism is proof of our love for Jesus and His love for us.

Food for Thought

God's love obligates us to love others. This is the supreme love of God.

DR. KENNETH HAROLD MCMILLAN

On Board

It is written that four men broke down barriers to get a paralytic close to Jesus. They were on a mission and were determined to accomplish it (Mark 2:1–17). We are also called to bring people to Jesus Christ. The physical condition, race, color, or creed should not be a barrier. We must do whatever is needed to break down barriers of any kind to bring or lead people to Christ.

These men could have left the paralyzed man to himself, ignoring him, implying it was God's job to save him. Instead, they carried him to Jesus.

Sin paralyzes. So many people are blinded by Satan and his devices. Christians are called to reach and teach the lost. God wants *all* aboard. *all* Christians are commissioned to bring *all* people to Jesus Christ. At times, we must take unusual and uncomfortable approaches in accomplishing this task. The men alluded to in the scripture could not carry the paralytic through the crowd, so they dismantled the roof to let him down so he would be close to Christ, where he obtained *results*!

Three people cannot carry a stretcher with a man on it. Four people are needed—one person at each end.

Likewise, it takes at least four qualities to bring one soul to Christ: confidence, compassion, courage, and collaboration. We must first have confidence in the Word of God, believing that we can reach the lost. We must also have compassion, which is major in bringing or leading the lost to Christ. We must genuinely care about the lost and show concern for whatever he or she is going through or has been through. Additionally, we must be "strong and of good courage" (Deuteronomy 31:6).

More importantly, we must work in collaboration with lost individuals. They must permit us into their world and develop some type association. They must have a willing mind, an ear to hear the Word, receptive hearts to receive Christ Jesus, and make a full confession for their sins and profession of their faith, stating they believe that Jesus was born of a virgin named Mary, suffered and died on the cross for the sins of mankind, and rose on the third day with all power in His hand.

Oftentimes, more than one person—perhaps four—may be needed in leading one soul to Christ, and it may be accomplished in stages. In this case, one of the four qualities must be dominant in each of the Christians approaching the lost, with the lost soul being willing to collaborate. We are to bring *all* people to Jesus Christ at *all* costs. This is the only way to obtain the desired *results—all aboard*.

Food for Thought

The church—the body of Christ—must do whatever it takes to get the lost on board with Jesus and obtain the *results* God requires.

Remember, it takes four:

- confidence
- compassion
- courage
- collaboration

Life Application

How willing are you to ensure that your family and friends know Jesus? _____

_____

_____

Is your "want to" in a place that compels you to reach lost souls? Explain. _____

_____

_____

DR. KENNETH HAROLD MCMILLAN

Obedience

Life Application

HAS THERE EVER been a point in your life that you were unhappy with your results and you had given the situation the best that you had to offer? Explain. _____

_____

_____

_____

- The resurrection of Jesus is paramount in the Gospel presentation. It represents the open door for the second coming of Christ Jesus and the blessed rapturing of Christ's church and His people. At this time, the people of God will receive the ultimate *results*!

- Jesus gave the command for the disciples to cast their nets into the deep. It appears that the Lord desires that we step outside of our comfort zone to do His bidding. This is where we live in God's overflow, where we obtain *results*.

- When we are obedient to God's call, the *results* and the outcome can be immediate and often overwhelmingly pleasing. Remember: the fishermen ended up with a multitude of fishes in a matter of minutes!

- The fishermen obeyed Christ and enjoyed tremendous success. The Lord rewards faithful, obedient servants. His promises are true!

- The number 153 represents the exact number of fish caught because of Jesus's miracle. It is significant to believers because every believer has been called to be a fisher of men, women, boys, and girls, and every soul is important to God.

- A belief is that Christ is challenging the modern-day church as he did with Peter. It is probable that He is challenging us to "let down our nets in the deep." We are called to go to unfamiliar places and reach out to people who have not heard of the Good news.

- When Jesus hosted a feast for His followers, all were invited. Likewise, we should follow in Jesus's footsteps and invite all our followers to come to Jesus.

- Christ is the ever-present provider for His people. We must learn to depend on Him to help us and supply all our needs.

Life Application

Why do some people get divine supplies and power and others do not? _____
_____
_____
_____

Read Philippians 4:19. What promise is contained in this scripture? _____
_____
_____
_____

DR. KENNETH HAROLD MCMILLAN

Conclusion: Stand Firm

CHRISTIANS ARE MOST effective in kingdom building when they remain focused on King Jesus. There is no substitute for prayer, the most powerful tool our God graciously gave to us. Nor is there a substitute for the Word of God, our blueprint for living. There are also no shortcuts regarding ministry. Ministry leaders, and believers in general, influence and impact others positively or negatively.

Food for Thought

Yesterday is gone. Yesteryear is gone. Today is here. Only God knows tomorrow.

Foundations for Life

- Search the scriptures. Allocate time to study the Word of God to obtain more wisdom, knowledge, and understanding.
- Apply the scriptures to life.
- Develop good habits. Let old habits go and ask (pray) for better ones.
- Do not give or use excuses. *Results* are what matter. Do away with distractions (people, places, and things). Never underestimate the significance of being obedient in matters that seem to be of little importance.
- Set attainable goals for yourself. The Word of God reminds us to not owe anybody anything other than love (Romans 13:8). We are admonished to leave no debt outside—to pay whatever was vowed. God grants greater responsibility to those who have been faithful with small things.
- Allocate time for families to reunite.
- Do what is necessary to acquire a closer relationship with Jesus.
- Remain humbled.
- Remain teachable.

- Do all things with eternity in view—not just for your sake, but for the sake of all under your influence.

Look to God for all answers; He is omniscient. He is also omnipotent; He is all powerful. We are the church, and we are commanded to take the message of Jesus and the Gospel outside the four walls.

ION = Results!

Integrity and

Obedience

Now.

DR. KENNETH HAROLD MCMILLAN